For Zachary, whose fantasy world
sent me on a quest of my own.

Design by Sean Yates

This Beowulf adaptation was originally published by qarrtsiluni.com and edited by Alex Cigale.

Published by Zouch Six Shilling Press
An imprint of Zouch Magazine
info@zouchmagazine.com

Printed in the U.S.A.



ISBN 978-0-9851754-2-9

# BEOWULF

A VERSE ADAPTATION WITH YOUNG READERS IN MIND

By Joshua Gray

Illustrations by
Sean Yates

IMAGINE: ◆ the long arctic night in a Viking ◆ longhouse; a large rectangular box stacked of rough-hewn, fitted logs, several families gathered around a fire blazing at its center under a smoke-hole, and on special nights, a feast of mead and meat, a saga recited, from memory of course, to the accompaniment of drum, pipe, or string, strung and strummed. Our very understanding of verse stems from this: stanzas of lines ("stich"), literally furrowed plots sown with letters instead of seeds, the four beats keeping steady the rise, draw, dip, and pull of oars in the long ships, the staccato alliteration or repetition of three consonants in each line an aide to memory so that the bard might recite for thousands of lines and history live without being written down and the deeds of heroes be made to live again in the human voice.

What makes Joshua Gray's "verse adaptation with young readers in mind" immediate and powerful is its tender tone: it is addressed to his son, in the same understated, hushed voice of expectation as a will and testament, that it contains a coded message to be passed down from the son, who is father to the man, to his own son and so on. Moreover, being written "with young readers in mind," and not "for young readers only," makes it truly special, for in making Beowulf more accessible he has done the time-honored service of digest and abridgement for busy adults as well, and in doing so has helped this reader for one focus on the story's essential message; that it's very telling—not just its symbolic content but the form itself—represents the eternal bond between fathers and sons and so between all men.

Divided as it is into 10 distinct stanzas or "chapters," a Table of Contents may be useful. Chapter 1 shows Hrothgar in his castle/hall, Heorot. From the very first lines, Gray's careful attention to retaining elements of the alliterative-accentual original are evident, as when the beast is introduced "called Grendel" who "was grand and gruesome." Chapter 2 is Beowulf's Back-story of Battles with Sea-Monsters. In Chapter 3 Beowulf Beats Grendel. Chapter 4 in which Grendel's Mother Gets her Revenge. In Chapter 5 Beowulf Returns to Deep Waters to Battle the Monster's Mother. Chapter 6 In which we learn what do when we think all is lost. Chapter 7 is Hrothgar's Fatherly Advice to Beowulf; or what your friends won't tell you. Chapter .8 Beowulf Returns Home and Becomes King of the Geats, but a Dragon... Chapter 9: Beware of Fighting Dragons Lest... Chapter 10 You become old and treasure-loving like them...

...but Youth Always Triumphs, and it all goes around again! To be politically correct, and morally relative, in the context of the Vikings, the great and eternal human values of Loyalty, Honor, Courage of Heart and Bravery in Action, of Generosity may be symbolized (as they are for that other infernally bankrupt and immensely popular "children's" genre, the Pirate Tale) by the Treasure Hoard, the product of a life of Raiding, but also a lasting image of age and wisdom and strength. This story for all ages, in every sense, will bring you and your child, without and within, between the ages of 4 and 84, closer together and will stand up to a lifetime or re-reading. LET THERE BE DRAGONS!

ALEX CIGALE: POET, EDITOR, TRANSLATOR, CYCLIST, SPIRIT/ROAD WARRIOR

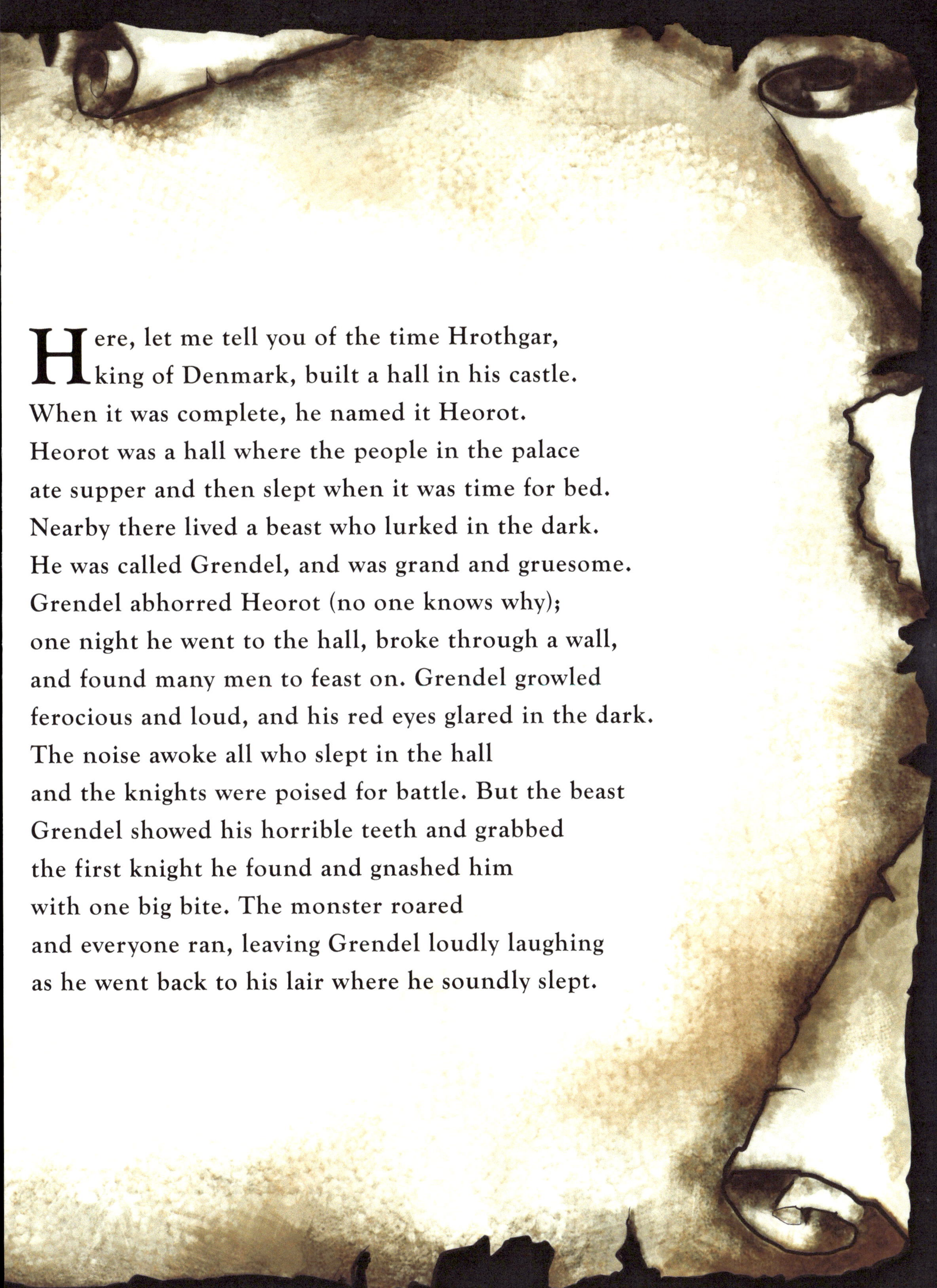

Here, let me tell you of the time Hrothgar,
king of Denmark, built a hall in his castle.
When it was complete, he named it Heorot.
Heorot was a hall where the people in the palace
ate supper and then slept when it was time for bed.
Nearby there lived a beast who lurked in the dark.
He was called Grendel, and was grand and gruesome.
Grendel abhorred Heorot (no one knows why);
one night he went to the hall, broke through a wall,
and found many men to feast on. Grendel growled
ferocious and loud, and his red eyes glared in the dark.
The noise awoke all who slept in the hall
and the knights were poised for battle. But the beast
Grendel showed his horrible teeth and grabbed
the first knight he found and gnashed him
with one big bite. The monster roared
and everyone ran, leaving Grendel loudly laughing
as he went back to his lair where he soundly slept.

The monster managed to raid Heorot for eleven years. Finally it became clear King Hrothgar needed help killing the beast in battle, because his warriors were dying one by one in this gruesome Grendel War. The Danes prayed to the gods to keep the monster from preying on them. Their prayers were answered when a ship sailed to their shores. Beowulf was aboard the boat, and he came from across the sea to help Hrothgar from the terror of Grendel's teeth. Beowulf announced himself to Hrothgar, and the King welcomed him with open arms. Hrothgar fed his guest a feast in his hall, and Beowulf announced he planned to fight Grendel with his fists. Unferth, Hrothgar's bravest knight, questioned Beowulf's skill. Unferth asked, "Are you the legendary Beowulf, who took part in a swimming contest with a friend in the ocean? As I have heard the story, you both challenged each other and the sea for seven nights, swimming as far out as you could, beating the cold and angry waves, but in the end your friend won the race, you fell behind humiliated." Beowulf balked. "You're right brave Unferth, I am that Beowulf. But you have heard wrong. For five days and nights we swam shoulder to shoulder against those cold and angry waves. I was pulled under by a sea-monster. Armed with a sword, I killed the sea-monster and eight others after it. It was a hard fight under water with those terrible beasts, and I was weakened but I swam to the surface and made it to the other shore. Not since my fight with the sea-monsters have my people perished at the mouths of them. I lost, but I was honored, not humiliated."

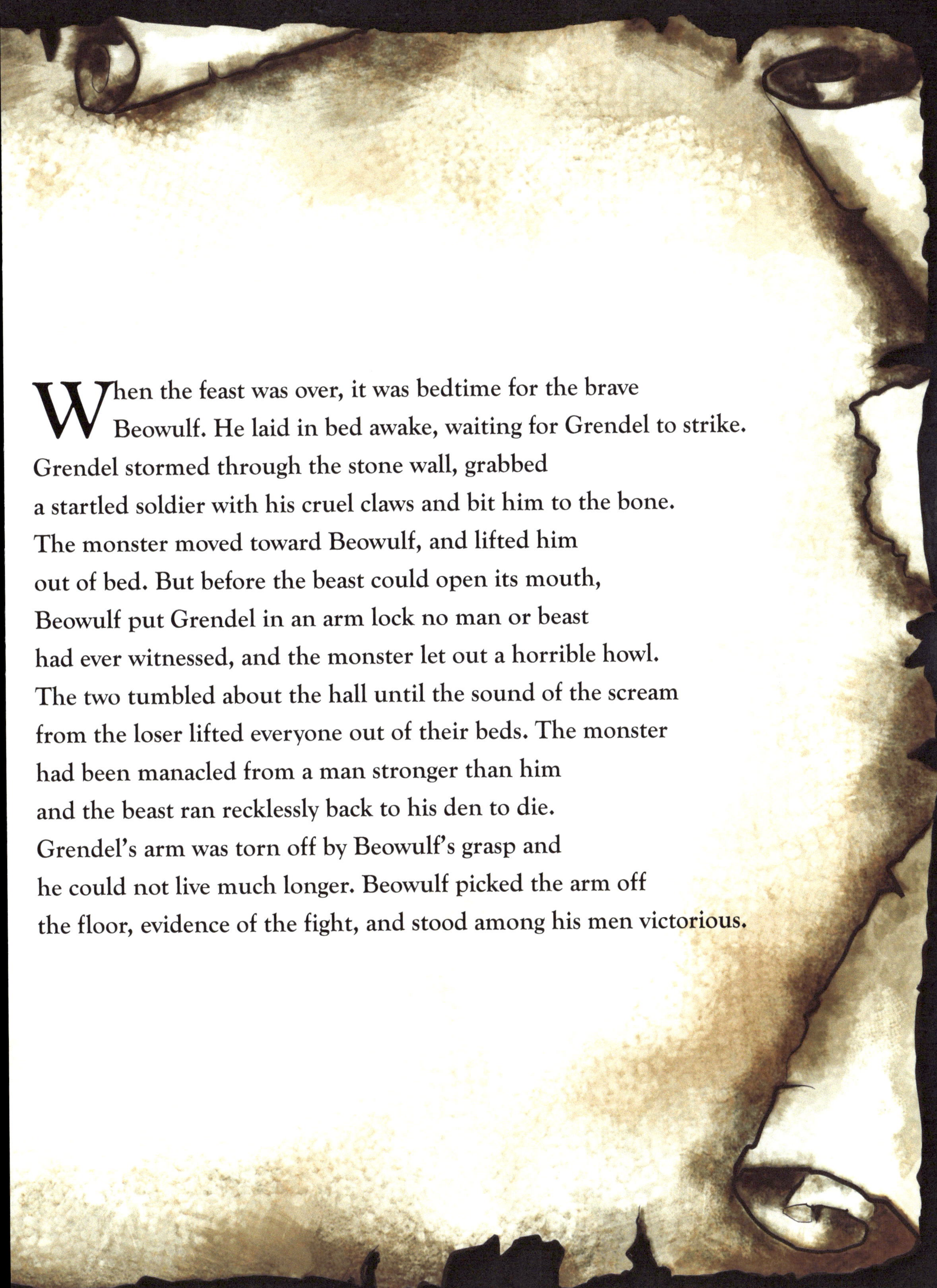

When the feast was over, it was bedtime for the brave Beowulf. He laid in bed awake, waiting for Grendel to strike. Grendel stormed through the stone wall, grabbed a startled soldier with his cruel claws and bit him to the bone. The monster moved toward Beowulf, and lifted him out of bed. But before the beast could open its mouth, Beowulf put Grendel in an arm lock no man or beast had ever witnessed, and the monster let out a horrible howl. The two tumbled about the hall until the sound of the scream from the loser lifted everyone out of their beds. The monster had been manacled from a man stronger than him and the beast ran recklessly back to his den to die. Grendel's arm was torn off by Beowulf's grasp and he could not live much longer. Beowulf picked the arm off the floor, evidence of the fight, and stood among his men victorious.

The next day word got around that the beast had been beaten by Beowulf. The damaged wall in the hall was repaired, and Hrothgar gave Beowulf gifts for his courage. A victory feast was served for supper, and everyone was the happiest they'd been since Grendel started running his raids. That night as they settled in for sleep, it felt great to not worry about Grendel again. Beowulf went to bed elsewhere. But as soon as everyone was asleep and silence swept the night, a second terror lurked in the moonlight. Grendel's mother had come to Heorot to avenge her son's death. She was just as gruesome as Grendel. The sleeping were startled awake, and they all went for their swords. Grendel's mother killed a counselor, Hrothgar's right-hand man. She grabbed Grendel's arm, gave an angry growl, and disappeared.

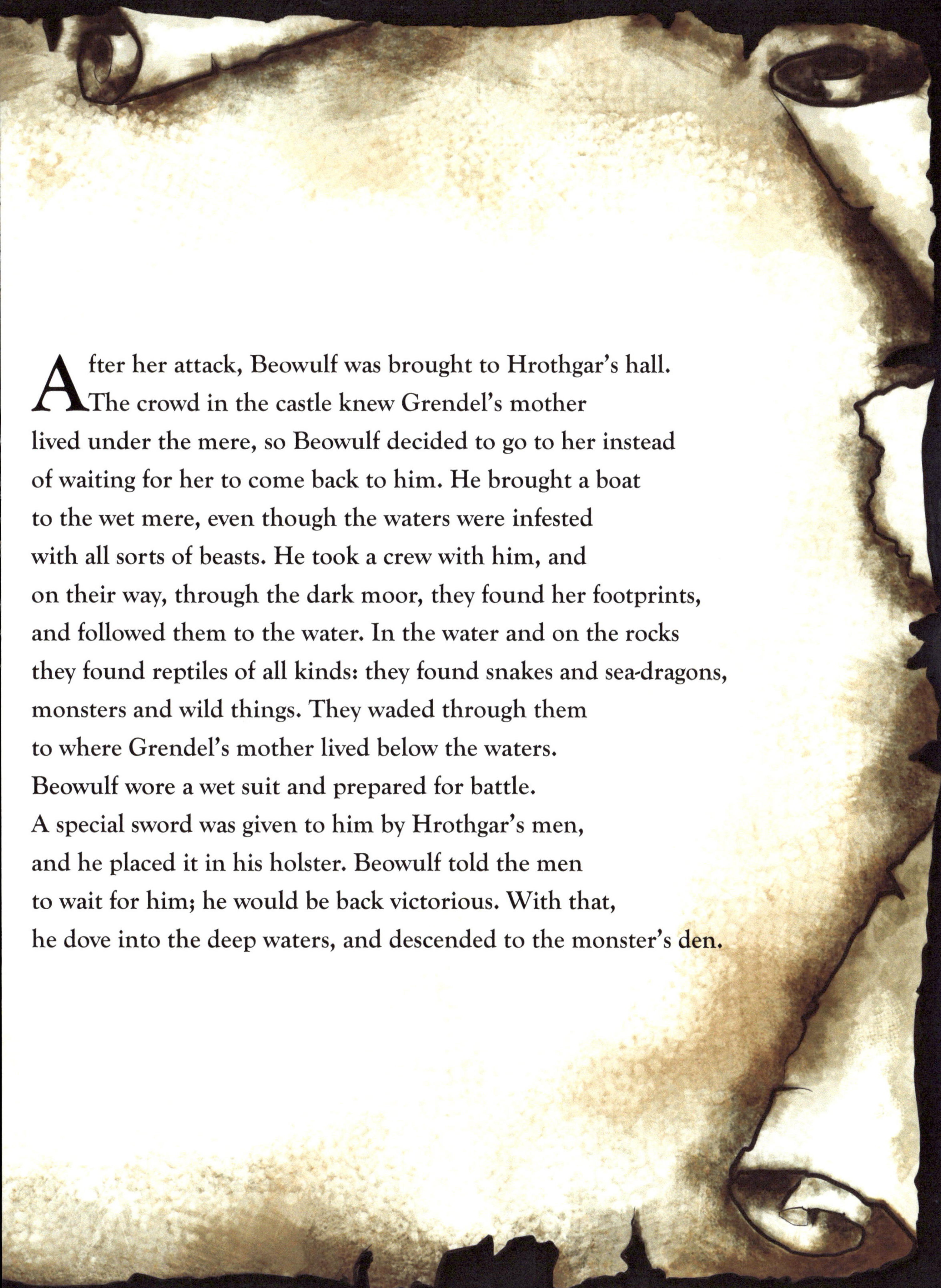

After her attack, Beowulf was brought to Hrothgar's hall. The crowd in the castle knew Grendel's mother lived under the mere, so Beowulf decided to go to her instead of waiting for her to come back to him. He brought a boat to the wet mere, even though the waters were infested with all sorts of beasts. He took a crew with him, and on their way, through the dark moor, they found her footprints, and followed them to the water. In the water and on the rocks they found reptiles of all kinds: they found snakes and sea-dragons, monsters and wild things. They waded through them to where Grendel's mother lived below the waters. Beowulf wore a wet suit and prepared for battle. A special sword was given to him by Hrothgar's men, and he placed it in his holster. Beowulf told the men to wait for him; he would be back victorious. With that, he dove into the deep waters, and descended to the monster's den.

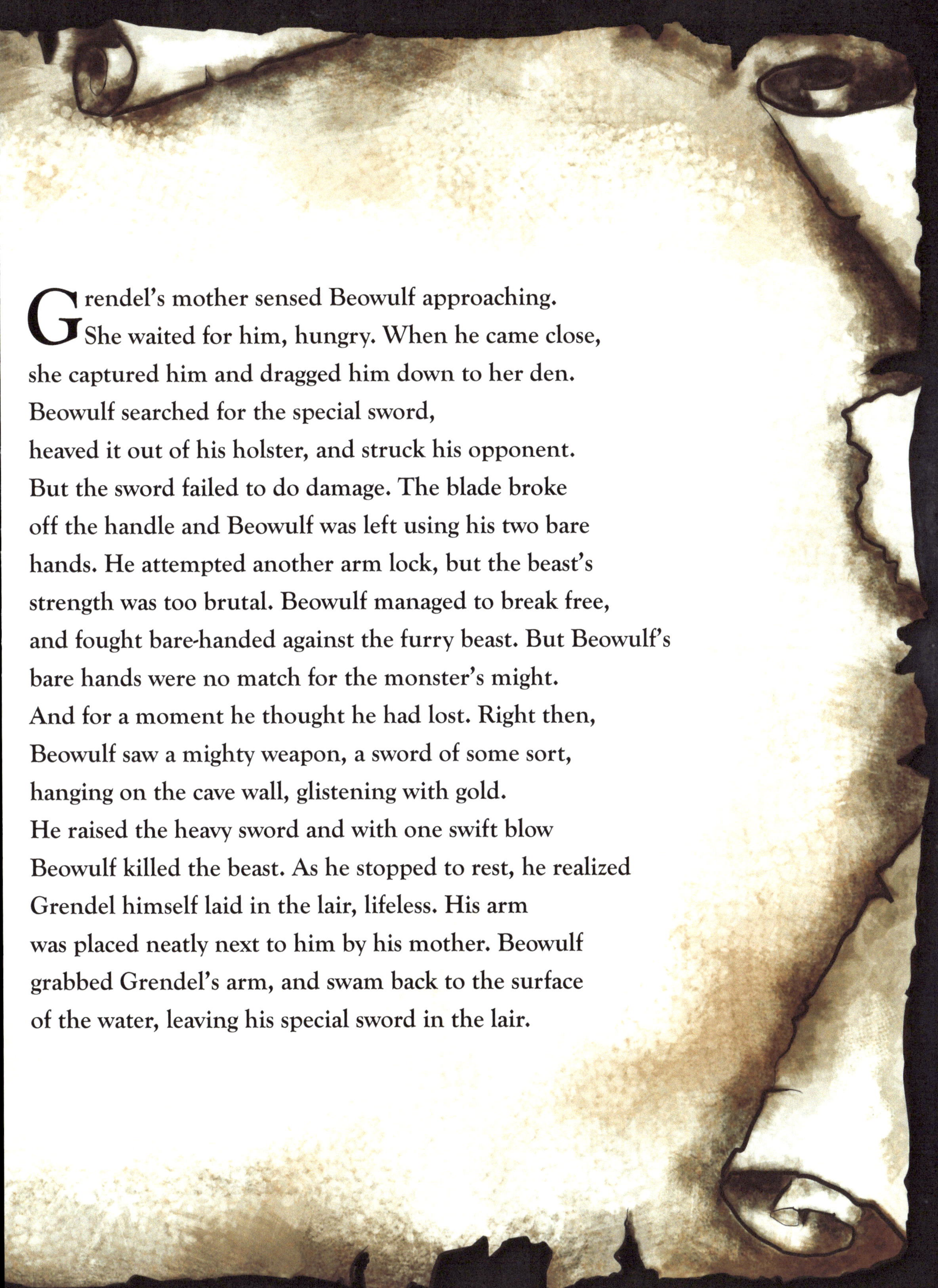

Grendel's mother sensed Beowulf approaching. She waited for him, hungry. When he came close, she captured him and dragged him down to her den. Beowulf searched for the special sword, heaved it out of his holster, and struck his opponent. But the sword failed to do damage. The blade broke off the handle and Beowulf was left using his two bare hands. He attempted another arm lock, but the beast's strength was too brutal. Beowulf managed to break free, and fought bare-handed against the furry beast. But Beowulf's bare hands were no match for the monster's might. And for a moment he thought he had lost. Right then, Beowulf saw a mighty weapon, a sword of some sort, hanging on the cave wall, glistening with gold. He raised the heavy sword and with one swift blow Beowulf killed the beast. As he stopped to rest, he realized Grendel himself laid in the lair, lifeless. His arm was placed neatly next to him by his mother. Beowulf grabbed Grendel's arm, and swam back to the surface of the water, leaving his special sword in the lair.

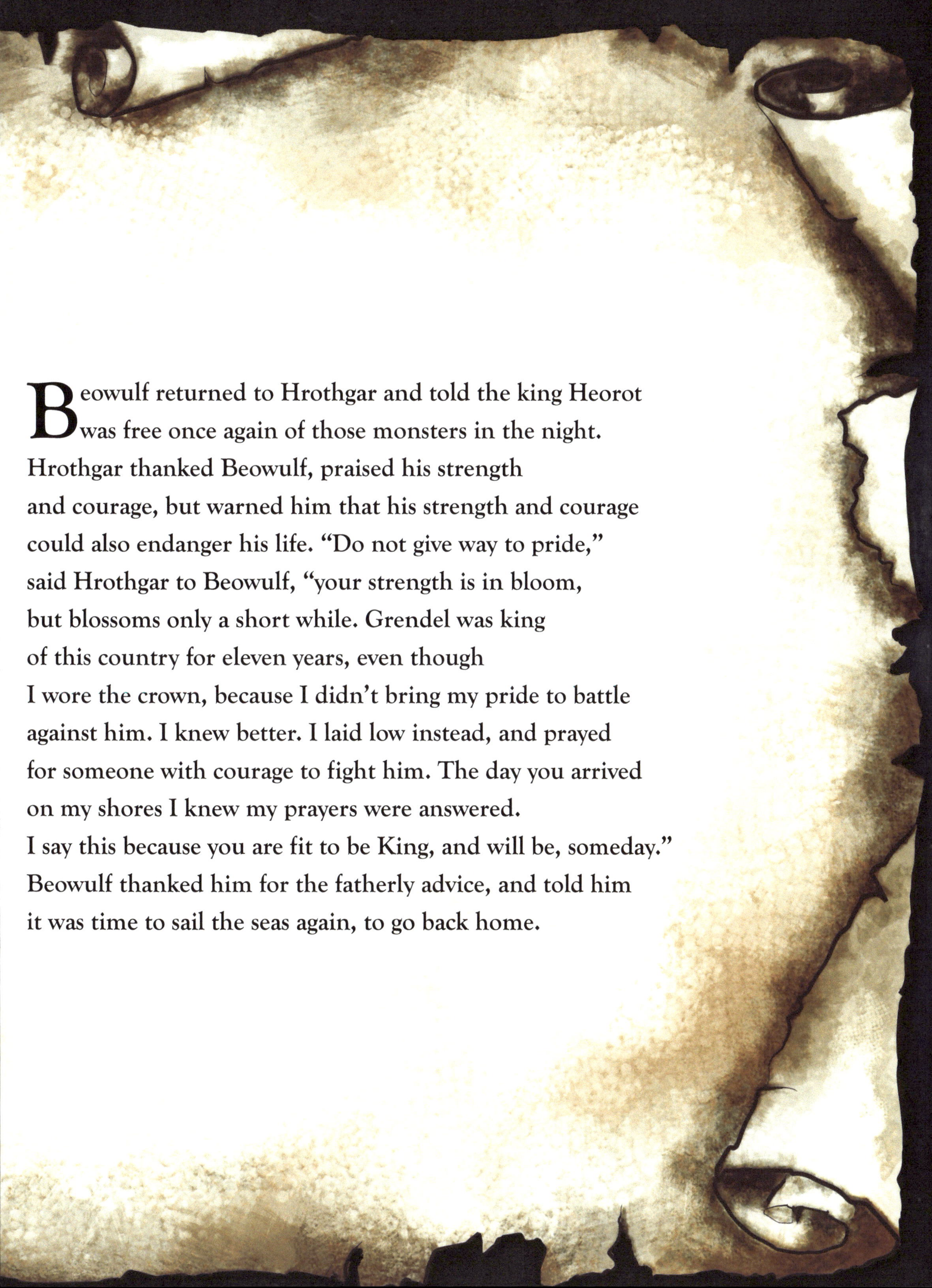

Beowulf returned to Hrothgar and told the king Heorot was free once again of those monsters in the night. Hrothgar thanked Beowulf, praised his strength and courage, but warned him that his strength and courage could also endanger his life. "Do not give way to pride," said Hrothgar to Beowulf, "your strength is in bloom, but blossoms only a short while. Grendel was king of this country for eleven years, even though I wore the crown, because I didn't bring my pride to battle against him. I knew better. I laid low instead, and prayed for someone with courage to fight him. The day you arrived on my shores I knew my prayers were answered. I say this because you are fit to be King, and will be, someday." Beowulf thanked him for the fatherly advice, and told him it was time to sail the seas again, to go back home.

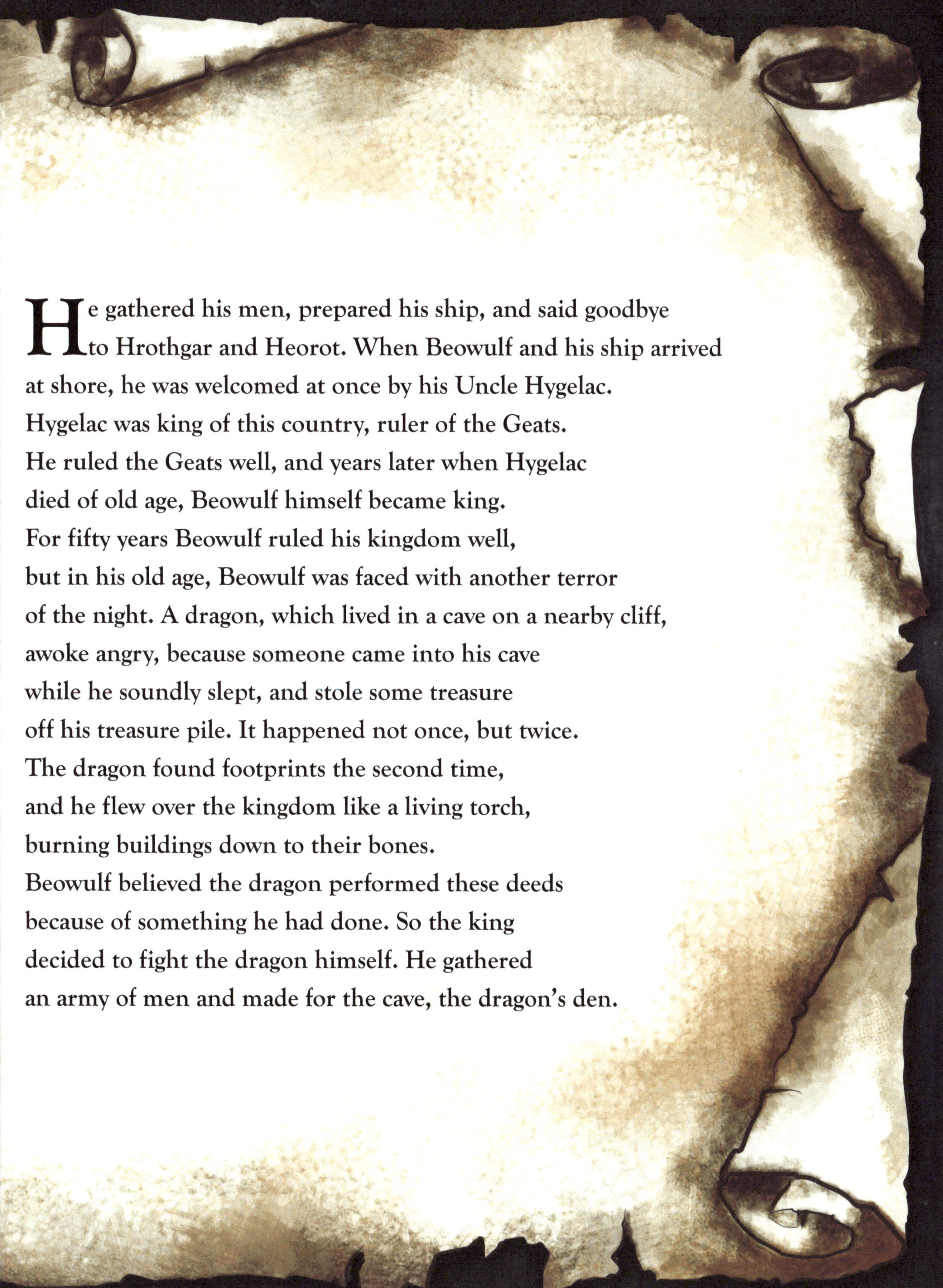

He gathered his men, prepared his ship, and said goodbye to Hrothgar and Heorot. When Beowulf and his ship arrived at shore, he was welcomed at once by his Uncle Hygelac. Hygelac was king of this country, ruler of the Geats. He ruled the Geats well, and years later when Hygelac died of old age, Beowulf himself became king. For fifty years Beowulf ruled his kingdom well, but in his old age, Beowulf was faced with another terror of the night. A dragon, which lived in a cave on a nearby cliff, awoke angry, because someone came into his cave while he soundly slept, and stole some treasure off his treasure pile. It happened not once, but twice. The dragon found footprints the second time, and he flew over the kingdom like a living torch, burning buildings down to their bones. Beowulf believed the dragon performed these deeds because of something he had done. So the king decided to fight the dragon himself. He gathered an army of men and made for the cave, the dragon's den.

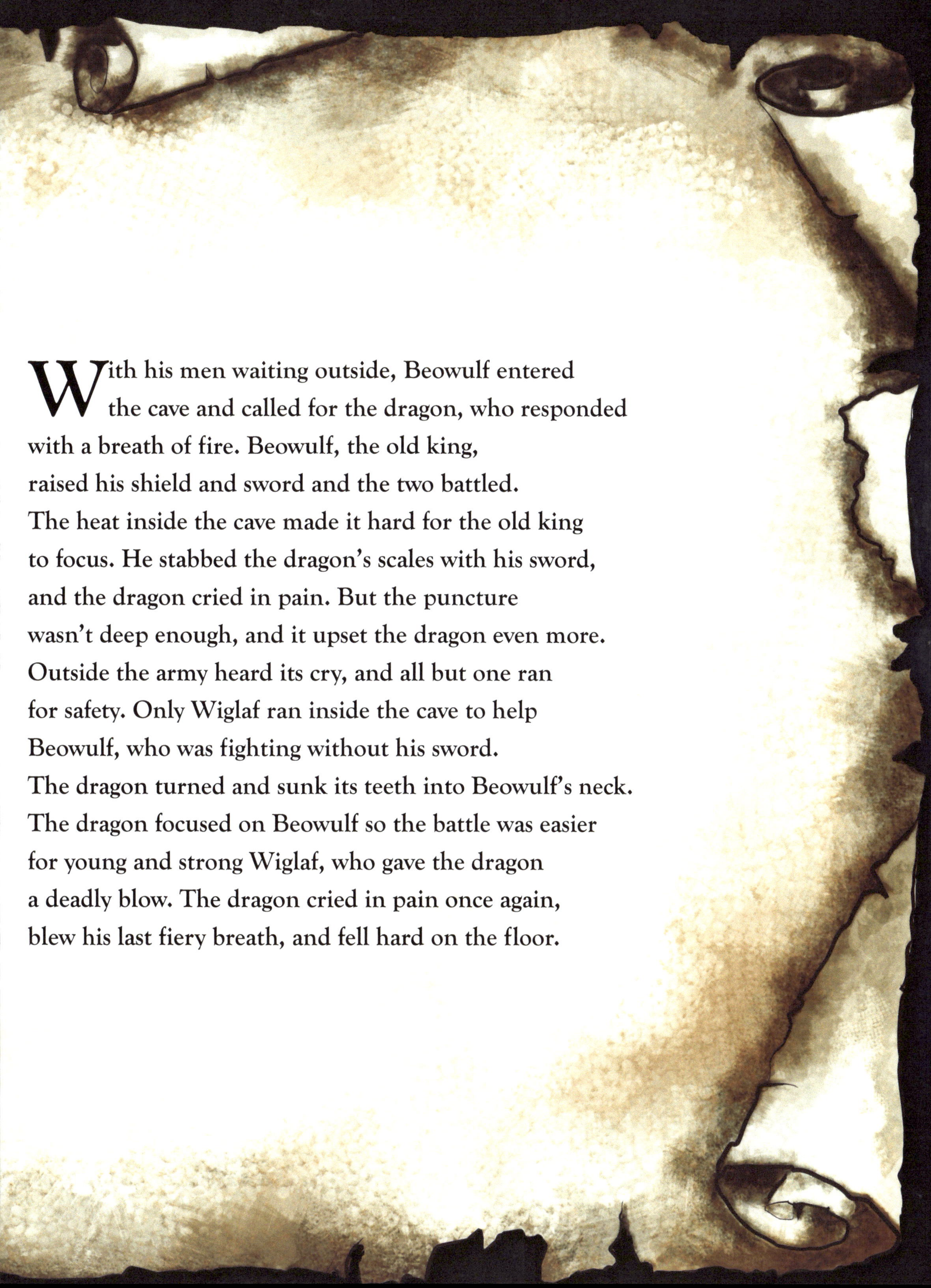

With his men waiting outside, Beowulf entered the cave and called for the dragon, who responded with a breath of fire. Beowulf, the old king, raised his shield and sword and the two battled. The heat inside the cave made it hard for the old king to focus. He stabbed the dragon's scales with his sword, and the dragon cried in pain. But the puncture wasn't deep enough, and it upset the dragon even more. Outside the army heard its cry, and all but one ran for safety. Only Wiglaf ran inside the cave to help Beowulf, who was fighting without his sword. The dragon turned and sunk its teeth into Beowulf's neck. The dragon focused on Beowulf so the battle was easier for young and strong Wiglaf, who gave the dragon a deadly blow. The dragon cried in pain once again, blew his last fiery breath, and fell hard on the floor.

Wiglaf ran to Beowulf's aid, and attempted to treat his wound. "Wiglaf," said Beowulf, "bring me some treasure, so I can see what I've been fighting for." Wiglaf ran around the fallen dragon, and fetched a piece of treasure, something simple he could carry. Beowulf's eyes fell on it. "Ah," he said, "Wiglaf, I name you the new king of the Geats, you have shown your courage. I will die of my wound." And soon, the old king closed his eyes, breathed his last breath, and peacefully passed away.

"This is a very straightforward departure from Joshua Gray's normal style, and quite effective, given the audience. I have read, edited and published selected [sic] of his works for a number of years, and I'm always taken by the rhythm, and the liquid feel of his lines. Much of his work has its roots in the classical, yet it is contemporary, and real."

– FREDERICK BRIDGER, EDITOR-IN-CHIEF OF FRONT RANGE REVIEW

"Joshua Gray's rendering of Beowulf for children is 'grand and gruesome,' just like the monster Grendel that stalks its lines. Gray captures both the fearsomeness of the poem's monsters and the artful alliteration of its Anglo-Saxon origins, while leaving out the long speeches that would turn away many young readers. Hook the kids with this version, and hope that they will return to the longer poem in later years."

– TOD LINAFELT, GEORGETOWN UNIVERSITY

"Joshua Gray's poetic re-telling of the Beowulf epic as a tale for children gets to the essence of the action with a use of modern English which is accessible and clear for young minds, listening while busily building their own image-worlds. My own experience is in telling this story to adults in a language they no longer understand, but I have the sense that this new text may well encourage very young listeners, years later (after their bedtime stories are a distant memory), to recall this tale with pleasure and to discover a vibrant curiosity to know more about the doings of Hrothgar, Grendel and Beowulf. It will serve as a wise and entertaining investment in keeping this important story alive and well in our culture's memory, as oral poetry and a fertile field for imagination, in both children and those who read to them."

– BENJAMIN BAGBY, PERFORMER OF BEOWULF IN THE ORIGINAL ANGLO-SAXON

Joshua Gray is a Washington DC native and earned his BA from Warren Wilson College in Asheville, NC. Determined to learn how to write poetry without attending an MFA program, he submerged himself into many different books that teach the craft. He wrote Beowulf after finding no other poetic interpretation of the epic for children and decided to write one himself so that his seven-year-old could enjoy the tale in a scaled-down Anglo-Saxon form. His current project is a book-length poem on belonging, which begins with sections written in Sanskrit, Anglo-Saxon, Blank and Welsh verse. He lives in Takoma Park, MD with his wife and two boys.

---

Sean Yates is a graphic designer, illustrator and artist whose art career began by customizing biker jackets for goths in Washington, DC and St. Louis during the 90's. Eventually, Sean took his work from jackets to canvases, and it's been down hill ever since. Sean lives in Washington, DC with his wife and what he believes to be the ghost of his dead cat.

joshuagraynow.com seanyatesart.com

www.ingramcontent.com/pod-product-compliance
Ingram Content Group UK Ltd.
Pitfield, Milton Keynes, MK11 3LW, UK
UKHW060122300726
14090UKWH00002B/318

* 9 7 8 0 9 8 5 1 7 5 4 2 9 *